ALY RAISMAN

BY MATT SCHEFF

SportsZone

An Imprint of Abdo Publishing
abdopublishing.com

abdopublishing.com

Published by Abdo Publishing, a division of ABDO, PO Box 398166, Minneapolis, Minnesota 55439. Copyright © 2017 by Abdo Consulting Group, Inc. International copyrights reserved in all countries. No part of this book may be reproduced in any form without written permission from the publisher. SportsZone™ is a trademark and logo of Abdo Publishing.

Printed in the United States of America, North Mankato, Minnesota
102016
012017

Cover Photo: Soeren Stache/picture-alliance/dpa/AP Images
Interior Photos: Julie Jacobson/AP Images, 4-5, 7, 20-21; Gregory Bull/AP Images, 6, 17, 19; Stephan Savoia/AP Images, 8-9; John Gaps III/AP Images, 10-11; Ronald Martinez/ Getty Images Sport/Getty Images, 12-13; Robin Alam/Icon SMI 164/Newscom, 14-15; Jeff Roberson/AP Images, 16; Bruce Chambers/ZumaPress/Newscom, 18; Charles Sykes/ Invision/AP Images, 22-23; Amy Sanderson/Cal Sport Media/AP Images, 24-25; Julio Cortez/ AP Images, 26-27; Andrey/AGIF/Rex Features/AP Images, 28-29

Editor: Chrös McDougall
Series Designer: Jake Nordby

Publisher's Cataloging-in-Publication Data

Names: Scheff, Matt, author.
Title: Aly Raisman / by Matt Scheff.
Description: Minneapolis, MN : Abdo Publishing, 2017. | Series: Olympic stars | Includes bibliographical references and index.
Identifiers: LCCN 2016951819 | ISBN 9781680785623 (lib. bdg.) | ISBN 9781680785906 (ebook)
Subjects: LCSH: Raisman, Aly, 1994- --Juvenile literature. | Women gymnasts-- United States--Biography--Juvenile literature. | Women Olympic athletes-- United States--Biography--Juvenile literature. | Olympic Games (31st : 2016 : Rio de Janeiro, Brazil)
Classification: DDC 794.44/092 [B]--dc23
LC record available at http://lccn.loc.gov/2016951819

CONTENTS

QUEEN OF THE FLOOR

US gymnasts were thriving at the 2012 Olympic Games in London, England. Aly Raisman had already won two medals. One of them was a gold medal in the team competition. Now it was on to her final event, the floor exercise final. Raisman honored her Jewish heritage with her music, "Hava Nagila."

FAST FACT

Aly Raisman dedicated the routine to 11 Israeli Jewish athletes who were killed in a terrorist attack at the 1972 Olympic Games in Munich, West Germany.

Aly Raisman completes a tumbling pass during the floor exercise finals at the 2012 Olympics.

FAST FACT
Raisman became the first US woman to win an Olympic gold medal on the floor exercise.

Raisman performs her floor exercise at the 2012 Olympics.

Raisman is known for her powerful tumbling. Her form is flawless. She always looks in control as she flips through the air. This performance was no different. The crowd looked on in awe as Raisman jumped, flipped, and tumbled across the mat. When it was over, her coach wrapped her in a giant hug. Raisman's score of 15.6 put her in first place, and nobody caught her. She had won another gold medal!

Raisman, *center*, shows her Olympic floor exercise gold medal.

7

Good Luck In London
Aly Raisman!

A sign in Needham, Massachusetts, to support Aly during the 2012 Olympics

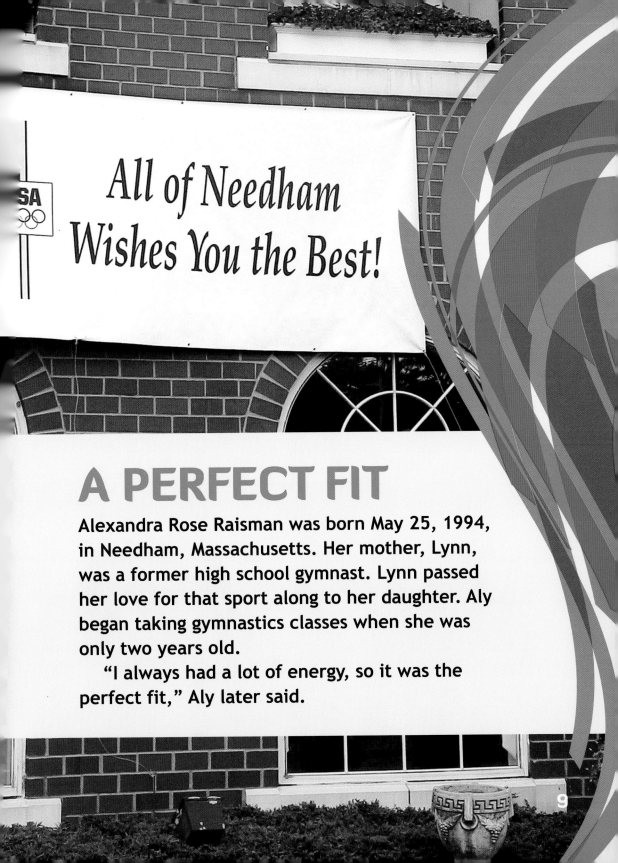

All of Needham
Wishes You the Best!

A PERFECT FIT

Alexandra Rose Raisman was born May 25, 1994, in Needham, Massachusetts. Her mother, Lynn, was a former high school gymnast. Lynn passed her love for that sport along to her daughter. Aly began taking gymnastics classes when she was only two years old.

"I always had a lot of energy, so it was the perfect fit," Aly later said.

Aly had more than just energy. She was a natural in the gym. Her parents saw her talent early on and signed her up for individual lessons. Soon she was taking part in local tumbling competitions.

The "Magnificent Seven" 1996 US women's gymnastics team

FAST FACT
As a child, Aly loved to watch videos of the 1996 US Olympic women's gymnastics team. The "Magnificent Seven" won the team gold medal.

Aly, *left*, and Alicia Sacramone at the 2011 US championships

Aly continued to build her skills. At 10 years old, she began training at Brestyan's American Gymnastics Club in Burlington, Massachusetts. She trained with fellow rising gymnastics star Alicia Sacramone. The older Sacramone became a mentor to Aly. She said Sacramone was like an older sister.

By 2009, 14-year-old Aly had made a name for herself as a junior. It was time to move on to the senior level.

FAST FACT

Alicia Sacramone was a member of the 2008 US Olympic team that won a silver medal.

Raisman competes on the balance beam at the 2011 US Classic.

STEALING THE SHOW

Aly Raisman made an instant impact at the senior level. She finished second in the all-around event at the 2010 American Cup. By 2011 her sights were set on the 2012 Olympics. Raisman left her high school to study online. That allowed her more time for training. She also became a professional, giving up her chance to compete in college.

"I just wanted to try it and have no regrets because I thought if I didn't try to go pro I'd always wonder," she said.

Raisman became
known for her
steady work on the
balance beam.

Raisman's hard work paid off. She made the 2012 US Olympic team. In July she traveled to London to compete on the sport's biggest stage. The United States had not won a women's team gymnastics gold medal since 1996. But many experts favored Team USA to win in 2012. As a natural leader, Raisman was named the team captain. It was her job to lead the way.

Gabby Douglas, *left*, and Raisman react after being named to the 2012 US Olympic team.

Raisman salutes after a balance beam performance at the 2012 Olympics.

FAST FACT
The 2012 US women's gymnastics team called themselves the "Fierce Five."

One by one, the US gymnasts performed excellent routines. Raisman was the last American to compete. The team gold medal was almost assured. Raisman needed to score only 10.234 on the floor exercise. That would be a very low score for Raisman. But her teammates still watched anxiously.

They had no reason to worry. Raisman struck her final pose. Everyone knew she had done it. Her teammates wrapped her in hugs. They were gold medalists! And they were not done yet.

The "Fierce Five" celebrates their Olympic gold medals.

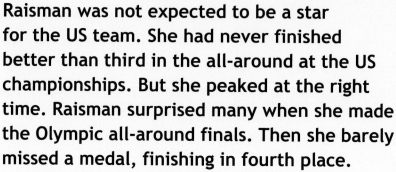

Raisman was not expected to be a star for the US team. She had never finished better than third in the all-around at the US championships. But she peaked at the right time. Raisman surprised many when she made the Olympic all-around finals. Then she barely missed a medal, finishing in fourth place.

Next she won a bronze medal in the individual balance beam competition. She finished with her amazing gold-medal performance on the floor exercise.

FAST FACT

Raisman actually tied for third place in the all-around. However, Aliya Mustafina of Russia won the bronze medal due to a tiebreaking rule.

Raisman completes a release move on the uneven bars during the 2012 Olympic all-around competition.

Raisman and her *Dancing with the Stars* partner perform on a morning show in 2013.

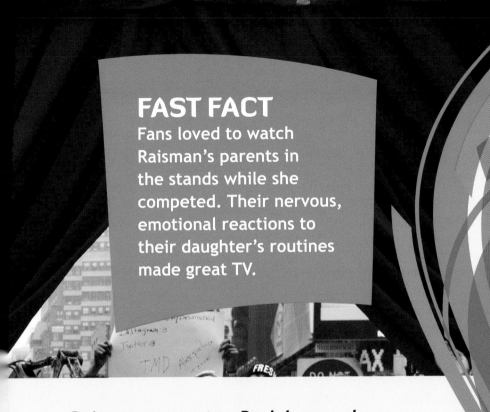

Raisman was a star. Back home, she enjoyed her fame and took some time off. She appeared on the popular TV show, *Dancing with the Stars*, in 2013. Raisman finished the competition in fourth place. But she still had a passion for gymnastics. Raisman knew she had more to prove. By 2014 it was back to training. It was time to prepare for the 2016 Olympics in Rio de Janeiro, Brazil.

NOT DONE YET

The United States is a gymnastics powerhouse. Each year talented new gymnasts join the senior ranks. Some fans wondered whether Raisman was too old to compete with the young stars. She quickly proved she could.

Raisman returned to competition in 2015. She finished third at the US championships. Then she helped Team USA win a gold at the World Championships. By the Olympic year in 2016, she was as good as she had ever been. When the Olympic team was announced, there was little surprise when Raisman's name was called.

Raisman, *right*, hugs teammate Laurie Hernandez at the 2016 US Olympic Team Trials.

FAST FACT

Raisman starred at the US Olympic Team Trials. She finished in the top three in the all-around, floor exercise, balance beam, and vault.

Raisman is known for being consistent. That continued at the Olympics in Rio de Janeiro. She competed in three of four events in team finals. Her scores helped Team USA win gold by more than eight points. And she was just getting started.

Next up was the all-around final. After 2012, Raisman left nothing to chance. Her score of 60.098 easily secured a silver medal. Raisman closed out the Olympic Games with another silver medal, this time in the floor exercise.

Raisman shined during the floor exercise in the 2016 Olympic all-around final.

Raisman waves to the crowd at the 2016 Olympics.

Raisman was not always the biggest star on the US team. Even in 2016, her teammate Simone Biles won four gold medals. But Raisman was always close to the top of the standings. She rarely made mistakes. And her floor exercise and balance beam routines were among the best in the world. So after being the oldest teammate on two Olympic squads, Raisman wants to do it again in 2020.

"I thought I was in the best shape of my life in 2012, but it's even better now," Raisman said after the 2016 Olympic Games. "I'm excited to see what can happen in 2020."

FAST FACT

After the 2016 Olympic Games, Raisman's total of six Olympic medals put her second on the all-time list for US gymnasts. Only Shannon Miller has more.

TIMELINE

1994
Alexandra Rose Raisman is born on May 25 in Needham, Massachusetts.

1996
The "Magnificent Seven" US women's gymnastics team wins an Olympic gold medal, inspiring Raisman to be a gymnast.

1996
Raisman begins taking gymnastics classes.

2003
Raisman begins training at Brestyan's American Gymnastics Club.

2010
Raisman begins senior-level competition. She finishes second in the all-around at the American Cup and makes her first World Championships.

2011
Raisman becomes a professional gymnast.

2012
Raisman earns three medals, including two gold, at the Olympics in London, England.

2013
Raisman competes on the TV show *Dancing with the Stars*.

2015
In her first year back competing, Raisman helps the US team win a gold medal at the World Championships.

2016
Raisman wins three medals at the Olympics in Rio de Janeiro, Brazil, including gold in the team competition.

GLOSSARY

all-around
A gymnastics competition in which women compete on all four events.

consistent
Able to perform in the same way over and over again.

dedicate
To perform in honor of someone or something.

heritage
the traditions, practices, or beliefs a group of people share.

junior
An elite female gymnast who is between 11 and 15 years old.

mentor
A person who helps teach and tutor a less experienced person.

professional
Someone who earns money for competing in a sport.

routine
A set performance by a gymnast on one event.

terrorist
Someone who uses violence to hurt and scare people in hopes of achieving a goal.

tumbling
Gymnastics elements such as flips and handsprings.

INDEX

About the Author

Matt Scheff is an artist and author living in Alaska. He enjoys mountain climbing, deep-sea fishing, and curling up with his two Siberian huskies to watch sports.